FOOTBALL

How to Play the All-Star Way

By **Dave Raffo**

Introduction by **Charles Johnson**

Illustrated by **Art Seiden**

Photographs by **Cliff Ginsburg**

★ An **Arvid Knudsen** book ★

RSVP
RAINTREE
STECK-VAUGHN
P U B L I S H E R S
The Steck-Vaughn Company

Austin, Texas

Acknowledgments: The photographs on pp. 6, 10, 24, 34, and 38 are from the collection of Mitchell B. Reibel. The photographs on pp. 4, 5, 8, 17, 18, 20, 27, 29, 32, 41, and 45 are from the collection of Arvid Knudsen & Associates.

Published by Raintree Steck-Vaughn Publishers, an imprint of Steck-Vaughn Company

Library of Congress Cataloging-in-Publication Data
Raffo, Dave.
Football/written by Dave Raffo.
p. cm.—(How to play the all-star way)
"An Arvid Knudsen book."
ISBN 0-8114-5780-X
1. Football—Juvenile literature. [1. Football.] I. Title.
II. Series.
GV950.7.R84 1994   93-23274
796.332—dc20   CIP AC

Printed and bound in the United States

1 2 3 4 5 6 7 8 9 0   99 98 97 96 95 94 93

CONTENTS

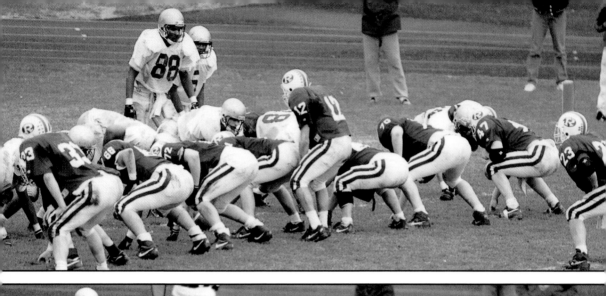

Coach Chuck Johnson

INTRODUCTION

Football is great fun to watch and play, but it is a demanding, rugged, contact sport. Therefore it is critical to learn how to play the game correctly. Only then will you be successful in the sport while having the most fun.

Playing correctly and using the proper equipment eliminates much of the physical risk associated with the game. Hours of practice and preseason workouts are required to achieve the necessary skills, discipline, and physical capabilities. Though most players do not play beyond their high school careers, the work ethic, teamwork, and character developed will stay with the athlete for the rest of his life. These traits are necessary for success in any sport, profession, or personal situation.

Football can be confusing to someone watching for the first time. This book will assist you greatly in the learning process as you become familiar with the mountain of terminology used by those close to the game. The diverse skill requirements of blocking, tackling, passing, kicking, catching, and running add to the game's sophistication.

Dave Raffo's book *Football: How to Play the All-Star Way* is a super introduction to this truly American game. GOOD LUCK!

— Charles Johnson,
Head Football Coach,
Ridgewood High School

◄ (Top) Quarterback receiving
ball from center
(Middle) Quarterback turns to
execute play
(Bottom) Ballcarrier is tackled
after small gain

A BIT OF FOOTBALL HISTORY

Football is very different today from what it used to be. The first football game was played in New Brunswick, New Jersey, in 1869. It was a college game between Rutgers and Princeton. In its early days football was more like soccer. But new rules changed the game. Players were allowed to carry the ball more. Later they were allowed to throw and catch the ball.

In the early days football was much rougher than it is today. It was almost outlawed because it was too rough. In 1905 alone 18 people were killed and 159 seriously injured while playing football. That was why the National Collegiate Athletic Association (NCAA) was formed. The association made new rules to make the sport safer. The forward pass was introduced. That made the game more exciting.

Great coaches like Knute Rockne, Amos Alonzo Stagg, John Heisman, and Glen "Pop" Warner helped football grow. They developed plays and strategies that made the game more interesting and less brutal. It required players to think more. Every fall, college football greats, like Red Grange and Jim Thorpe, provided thrills and excitement for the fans.

◀ Superstar Joe Namath led the underdog New York Jets to victory over the Baltimore Colts in the Super Bowl on January 12, 1969.

Pro Football

In 1920 the first professional league—the American Professional Football Association—was formed. Two years later the National Football League replaced it. Most of the teams in the new league were from the middle part of the country.

College football was more popular than professional football until the late 1950s. Then television made pro football more popular. In 1958 a large national television audience watched one of the most exciting NFL championship games ever played. Quarterback Johnny Unitas led the Baltimore Colts to a 23-17 victory over the New York Giants in overtime. It was the first championship game that ever had to go into overtime because it was tied at the end of the game. Even today, some people still call that 1958 championship game "the greatest game ever played."

Pro football became even more popular in the 1960s. There were exciting players, like Johnny Unitas, Jim Brown, Gale Sayers, Paul Hornung, and Joe Namath, and great coaches, like Vince Lombardi and Tom Landry. Their faces on TV every weekend helped make

football the country's most popular team sport. Professional football teams passed the ball more often than college teams did. That made pro games more exciting to watch.

By the 1970s, millions of Americans were watching pro football on television every weekend. Football stars, like Joe Montana, John Elway, Lawrence Taylor, and Barry Sanders, got paid millions of dollars. They became as famous as movie stars, top entertainers, and politicians.

The first Super Bowl was in 1967. It matched the champion of the NFL with the champion of the newer American Football League (AFL). In 1970, the AFL joined the NFL in a combined new pro league (NFL) that was divided into the American and National Football Conferences. The AFC and NFC champions meet every January in the Super Bowl. Every year the game is played in a different city. The Super Bowl has become America's favorite single-day sporting event.

College, High School, and Pop Warner Football

The big-college "bowl" games are played on or just before New Year's Day. There is no college championship game like the Super Bowl. The NCAA thinks college student-athletes should not have to face the pressure that such a championship game would bring.

The major college bowls are the Orange Bowl, Sugar Bowl, Cotton Bowl, Rose Bowl, and Fiesta Bowl. After the bowl games are over, coaches and sportswriters choose a national champion. Sometimes different polls choose different national champions.

High school seasons vary from state to state. They usually start in late September and run until Thanksgiving Day or shortly after. Many states now have high school play-off and championship games.

Players 7 to 15 years old can play in Pop Warner Leagues. These Pop Warner leagues are the football equivalent of Little League baseball. They are organized by age and weight so players play against opponents of similar age and size.

◄ Many states have high school play-offs and championship games.

BASIC EQUIPMENT

Football players wear more equipment than other athletes. They wear pads almost all the way from head to toe. The main pieces of football equipment are helmets, mouthpieces, shoulder pads, elbow pads, knee pads, hip pads, rib pads, thigh pads, athletic supporters, and football shoes. Football equipment makes players safer and helps them play better.

One important thing to remember about your equipment is that it should fit snugly. Loose helmets and pads can cause injuries. They also keep you from playing your best.

Helmets should not move from side to side. It is best to get a haircut before you are fitted for a helmet. If you get your hair cut after you are fitted for a helmet, the helmet will be loose. Always keep your chin strap buckled. Also, keep your mouthpiece connected to your face mask.

Mouthpieces are important. You should keep your mouthpiece in your mouth from the time you leave the huddle until the play ends. When you buy a new mouthpiece, take it home and wear it around the house for a few hours to break it in.

Shoulder pads should feel comfortable. They should be tight but not pinch. If they are too big, they will keep you from doing your

◄Dan Marino, quarterback for the Miami Dolphins, has the NFL's greatest passing arm.

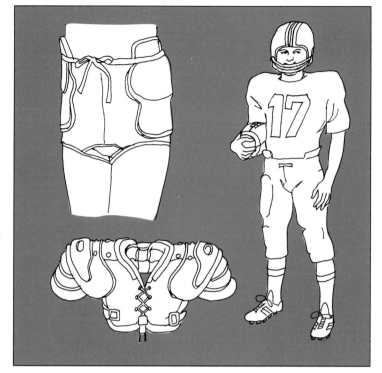

Thigh pads

Shoulder pads

Football uniform

best. Shoulder pads are important since most contact is made with the shoulders first.

Jerseys and pants should also be tight. But they should not be so tight that they are uncomfortable or slow you down. Put your jersey on over your shoulder pads before you decide if the jersey fits. Also, put your pants on with the thigh, knee, and hip pads on to make sure your pants fit. An athletic supporter and cup are important for all male football players.

You may or may not decide to wear forearm, elbow, knee, or rib pads. If they feel uncomfortable, you are probably better off doing without them. However, it is usually a good idea to wear rib pads to keep your ribs from getting cracked.

The shoes you wear will depend on what surface your team plays on. Some cleats are best for grass, others for artificial turf. Ask your coach what shoes you should buy.

Physical Conditioning

Getting into shape is important for two reasons: out-of-shape athletes do not perform as well, and they are more likely to be injured. Getting into shape and staying there is a year-round job. The best way to stay in shape for football is to play other sports the rest of the year. Track-and-field events are especially good for conditioning. The outdoor track-and-field season is in the spring, so it does not overlap with football. You also can stay in shape by playing tennis, racquetball, handball, and volleyball.

Lifting weights is also good. But don't begin lifting weights until you are at least 12 years old. Young players can get just as much out of push-ups, sit-ups, chin-ups, and rope climbing.

You can stay in shape in your own living room. Herschel Walker is a running back who won the Heisman Trophy in 1982 and went on to star in the NFL. At home Walker does hundreds of push-ups and sit-ups when he watches TV at night. He is as muscular and is in as good shape as any player who lifts weights.

Neck exercises are very important. A strong neck protects you against serious injury from a hard blow to the head. Your chest, shoulders, arms, stomach, and legs also need to be built up by weight training or exercise.

Conditioning exercises are a big part of preseason football practice. Running and stretching should be part of every workout. Conditioning exercises that begin in training camp should continue throughout the season.

Remember to get a complete physical checkup before the start of every season. Your school or town team may give you one. If not, go to your family doctor.

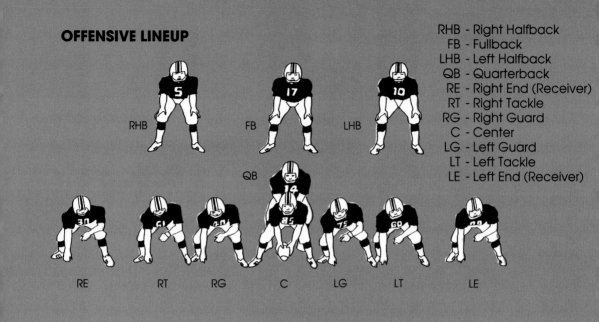

OFFENSIVE LINEUP

RHB
FB
LHB
QB
RE
RT
RG
C
LG
LT
LE

RHB - Right Halfback
FB - Fullback
LHB - Left Halfback
QB - Quarterback
RE - Right End (Receiver)
RT - Right Tackle
RG - Right Guard
C - Center
LG - Left Guard
LT - Left Tackle
LE - Left End (Receiver)

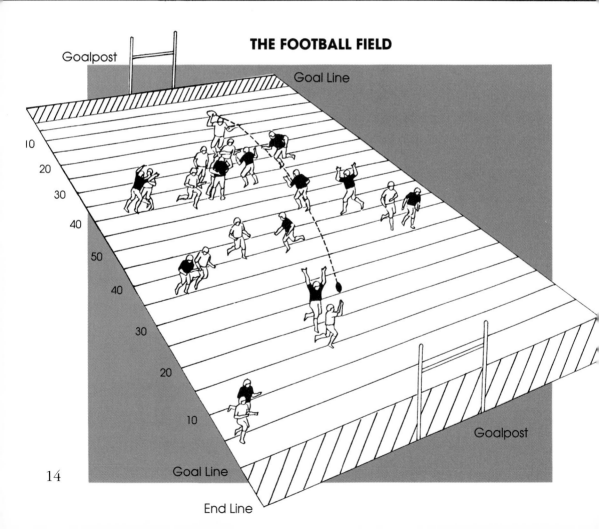

THE FOOTBALL FIELD

Goalpost

Goal Line

10
20
30
40
50
40
30
20
10

Goalpost

Goal Line

End Line

14

CHAPTER

3

HOW FOOTBALL IS PLAYED

A football field is 100 yards long and 53 1/3 yards wide. The 50-yard line in the middle of the field is called midfield. The yard lines on each side of the field are numbered from 1 to 49. They are usually marked off by white lines every 5 or 10 yards. Behind each goal line there is a 10-yard end zone. Goalposts are at the back of the end zone.

The Players

A football team has three units—an offensive team, defensive team, and special teams. During the game, each team has 11 players on the field.

The offense is the team with the ball. It tries to score a touchdown by crossing the goal line with the ball either by running or passing. The other team is called the defense. It tries to stop the offense by tackling the ballcarrier, knocking the ball loose for a fumble, or by knocking down or intercepting a pass. If a defensive player recovers a fumble or intercepts a pass, he can run the ball back toward the other team's goal line just like an offensive player. When that happens, players on the other team turn into tacklers who try to stop the player with the ball.

Special teams are used to kick off, punt, and receive kickoffs and punts. A special team on offense may kick the ball off, kick it through the goalposts for points, or punt it to the other team. A special team on defense is used to return kickoffs and punts. Punt and kickoff returns are often among the most exciting plays in football.

Every player is important to his team. Each player has a special job to do on every play. On the best teams players work together, so teamwork is very important.

Scoring

A touchdown is worth 6 points. It can be scored by any player who carries the ball over the goal line, catches a pass in the end zone, or recovers an opponent's fumble in the end zone.

Most touchdowns are scored by the offensive team. But a defensive player can also score a touchdown. He can recover a fumble or intercept a pass and run with the ball over the goal line. Special team players can also return kickoffs and punts for touchdowns.

After a team scores a touchdown, the team is allowed another play from the 3-yard line to get one or two extra points. A team gets one extra point if it kicks the ball through the goalposts. In the Pop Warner League, high school, and college, a team gets two extra points if it runs or passes the ball over the goal line. An NFL team only gets one point.

There are two other ways of scoring—field goals and safeties. A field goal—worth 3 points—is scored by kicking the ball through the goalposts. Field goal kickers get few chances to kick during a game. Still, they can make more of a difference between winning and losing than any other player.

Look at the 1990 New York Giants. In the NFL National Conference championship game, Matt Bahr kicked a 42-yard field goal as time ran out for a 15-13 victory over the San Francisco 49ers. Then, in the Super Bowl, the Giants defeated the Buffalo Bills 20-19 when the Bills' Scott Norwood missed a 47-yard field goal try in the final seconds. After three hours of exciting football, the two most

The object of the offense is to score.

important games of the season came down to field goal kicks in the final seconds.

A safety is scored when a defensive player tackles the ballcarrier behind the ballcarrier's goal line. A safety—worth 2 points—happens less often than any other scoring play.

Coaches

Football coaches have many different jobs. They teach the game and the skills it takes to play it. They set rules and keep discipline. They inspire their team and make it want to win. During the game itself they coach the team from the sideline. They call plays and decide formations. They substitute players into the game and make sure their players know what's going on.

For Pop Warner League and high school coaches, teaching is very important. Their players are still learning the game. Coaches want their players to play the game as effectively and safely as possible. Teaching the right way to block and tackle is especially important. Learning correct skills cuts down on the chance of injury. So does good conditioning. Coaches are also important role models for their players. They teach sportsmanship and inspire confidence in their young players.

Football coaches give "pep talks" to their players to make them want to win. The most famous talk by a coach to his players was the "Win One for the Gipper" speech Knute Rockne gave his Notre Dame team in 1928. Rockne's team was losing at halftime to a powerful Army team. In the locker room he told his players to win the game for "The Gipper." The Gipper was a former Notre Dame player who had died eight years earlier. Sure enough, Notre Dame went back out on the field and beat Army 12-6. It was one of the most talked about games in college football history.

In college football and the NFL, strategy is important for winning games. College and NFL coaches work long hours. Sometimes they might sleep in their office after a long night of watching game films. Watching films of earlier games helps them correct their team's mistakes. Offensive and defensive game plans are part of a team's strategy. Game plans are the plays and formations a coach thinks will work best against the next opponent.

Officials

Football officials serve as the game's policemen. They are easy to see because they usually wear striped shirts. The number of officials in a game varies from two or three in the Pop Warner Leagues to six or more in the NFL. Officials give penalties to players who break the rules. They place the ball down in the right position before every play. Officials also keep track of the down, the score, and the time left in the quarter. The head official is called the referee.

The referee is the boss of the field.

Timing

All football games are divided into four quarters. College and NFL quarters are 15 minutes long. High school quarters are usually 12 minutes long. A quarter in a Pop Warner League may be as short as 8 minutes.

The game clock keeps track of the time. It stops after incomplete passes, plays that end up out-of-bounds, and after touchdowns and field goals. At the end of the second quarter, there is a halftime. At halftime, the teams leave the field for 15 minutes or so. The third quarter then begins with a new kickoff.

The team with the most points at the end of the fourth quarter wins the game. The game ends in a tie if both teams have the same number of points. In the NFL a tie game is decided by playing an extra "sudden death" quarter. Sudden death means the first team to score points wins the game.

Beginning the Game

Each game begins with a kickoff. The teams line up on opposite sides of the field. The ball is placed on a tee on the kicking team's 35-yard line. When the whistle blows to start the game, the kicker runs up to the ball and kicks it toward the other team's goal line. Any player on the receiving team may catch the ball and run it back. The receiving team begins its offensive plays where the ballcarrier was tackled.

Kicking off and punting are two jobs for the kicker.

Teams kick off after they score a touchdown or field goal. They also kick off to start the second half. The team that received the ball to begin the game is the one that kicks off to start the second half.

Moving the Ball

The yard line where each play begins is called the line of scrimmage. The offense begins with a first down, or play. It must move the ball at least 10 yards in four downs to keep the ball. If the offense makes its 10 yards, it gets another four downs to make another 10 yards.

Sometimes touchdowns are scored on a long run or pass. But most scoring is done when a team moves the ball by getting first downs. A series of plays that moves the ball in this way is called a drive. If the drive ends in a touchdown or field goal, it is called a scoring drive.

A team that does not move the ball 10 yards in four plays has to give the ball up to the other team. The other team then gets the ball on the yard line where the first team was stopped. The play a team chooses depends on what down it is and how many yards it needs for a first down.

First down plays are usually running plays. They are a safer way of gaining ground. Sometimes a team will try a pass on the first down to surprise the other team. On second and third downs teams often pass if they need more than 5 yards to pick up a first down.

Most fourth down plays end in either a punt or field goal try. The offense will usually punt if it is on its own end of the field. It punts because it doesn't want to give the ball up to the other team close to its goal line.

A punt is a kick to the other team from behind the line of scrimmage. A player on the other team may return a punt like a kickoff. Sometimes a team that is losing late in the game may "go for it" on the fourth down. It will try to pick up the first down rather than punt. However, if it does not get the first down, the ball will go over to the other team.

An offensive team close to the other team's goal line will often try a field goal on the fourth down. If the kicker succeeds in kicking the ball through the goalposts, his team gets three points.

Offensive Plays

Both the offense and defense have a huddle before each play. In the huddle the players decide what they are going to do on the next play. In an offensive huddle the quarterback calls the next play. In a defensive huddle the captain of the defense usually decides on the formation for the next play.

The player calling the play stands or kneels in the middle of a circle of his teammates. Or he may face his teammates who line up in two rows. Sometimes the coach will call the next play. He will either send in a substitute with the play or signal it with his hands.

There are four basic running plays—the dive, off tackle, sweep, and draw. A dive is a run straight into the middle of the opponent's line. An off tackle is a run between the tackle and end. A sweep is a run around the end of the line. A draw is a trick play. The quarterback surprises the defense by pretending he is going to throw a pass. He then hands the ball off to a running back.

On a pass play, the quarterback throws the ball from behind the line of scrimmage. If the receiver catches the ball, he runs with it until he gets tackled. If the receiver does not catch the ball, it is ruled an incomplete pass. The ball then goes back to the line of scrimmage and gets set for the next play.

◄ Moving the ball takes full team effort.

Always catch the ball
with the hands.

An interception is when a defensive player catches a pass. This is called a turnover. A player who intercepts a pass can run the ball back toward the opposing goal line. A defensive player can also recover a fumble. A fumble happens when the ballcarrier loses control of the ball before he is tackled. Any player on the field can recover a fumble by diving on it or picking it up. The team that recovers the fumble gets possession of the ball.

The offense often will gain more yards by passing than by running. But throwing a pass can be dangerous. The defense can intercept the pass or tackle the quarterback behind the line of scrimmage. That's called a sack. Since quarterbacks usually drop back at least 5 yards to pass, sacks usually cause big losses. A big loss from a sack can kill a drive.

Penalties

Officials call a penalty when a player breaks a rule. Officials signal a penalty by blowing a whistle or dropping a handkerchief (called a penalty flag). There are penalties for lining up offsides, moving before the ball is snapped, blocking below the waist or from behind (called clipping), using hands illegally, pass interference, holding on offense, and unsportsmanlike conduct.

An offsides penalty is called when a player moves over the line before the play begins. Holding is when an offensive player grabs and holds onto his opponent. Pass interference is when a defensive player touches a receiver before the pass comes. Unsportsmanlike conduct is called for fighting, hitting an opponent after a play, throwing equipment, or using foul language. Penalties can cost a team 5, 10, or 15 yards.

THE REFEREE'S SIGNALS

Delay of game

Personal foul

Illegal kicking, batting, or touching the ball

Unsportsmanlike conduct

Clipping

Roughness and piling on

Anthony Munoz, a 10-time Pro Bowl offensive tackler for the Cincinnati Bengals, believes blockers should always attack.

PLAYING POSITIONS

It is a cool October afternoon. You are lined up at one end of the field. You are in your uniform with your teammates waiting for the kickoff. You think how great it would be to run downfield and make the first tackle of the game. Or maybe you are at the other end of the field waiting to receive the kick. You are excited. You are nervous. There are "butterflies" in your stomach. The kicker runs to the ball and kicks it. This is the moment you have been waiting for. You are playing football!

Now you are your team's center. You come out of the huddle and bend down over the ball. You wait for the quarterback to give the signal. You snap the ball back to him. Then you block the player in front of you.

Or you are the quarterback. You call the play in the huddle. You give the signal and get the ball from the center. You can either run with it, hand it off to a teammate, or throw a pass. Everybody is trying to figure out what you are going to do. You like the feeling of being in charge. You want to move your team down the field and score a touchdown.

Maybe you are a running back. You are in the backfield waiting for the quarterback's signal. You will take the ball from him and charge through the line. Or you may catch a short pass from the quarterback and take off toward the sidelines. You want to break into the open. Your only thought is to score a touchdown.

Maybe the other team has the ball and you are on defense. You are in the line looking at the big, strong player in front of you. He is going to do everything he can to block you out of the play. You want to rush past him so you can tackle the runner. Or you may rush the quarterback. You are going to try to "sack" him before he throws his pass.

That is the thrill and fun of football. To find out what position will be best for you, let's learn more about them.

Offense

The two teams on the field are the offense and defense. The offense is the team with the ball. The offensive team tries to move the ball

Fumble

against the defense. The defensive team tries to keep the offense from moving down the field and scoring a touchdown. The offense is made up of a backfield, a line, and receivers.

Backfield

The quarterback and running backs make up the backfield. They begin each play behind their offensive line. The job of the line is to protect the backfield to keep the defense from tackling the quarterback or running backs.

26

Quarterback. The quarterback is the most important player on offense. He handles the ball on just about every play. The quarterback should have a good passing arm. He should also be able to find open receivers when they run out for a pass. On Pop Warner, high school, and some college teams, the quarterback also needs to be a good runner. NFL coaches don't like their quarterbacks to run with the ball. They can get hurt when they are tackled. But pro quarterbacks should be fast enough to get away from charging linemen and others coming at them.

Tall quarterbacks have an easier time seeing over the other players when they throw a pass. Some of the best pro quarterbacks are big, strong-armed passers like John Elway of the Denver Broncos and Dan Marino of the Miami Dolphins. But you can be a good quarterback without being big or strong.

For example, superstar Joe Montana is shorter than most quarterbacks and does not throw the ball as far as many NFL passers. Still, he led the San Francisco 49ers to four Super Bowl titles in the 1980s. Joe Montana is proof that brains, a strong desire, and determination to win are what count.

The quarterback is the leader of the offense. In the huddle the quarterback calls the play. That means he tells the rest of his team what the play is going to be. The quarterback also gives the "snap count." That tells his teammates on what count the center will snap the ball to begin the play.

Halfback. Halfbacks run with the ball more than anybody else. In some offenses the halfback is also called the tailback. Halfbacks have to be able to run fast and change direction quickly to keep from being tackled. They catch passes, too. Halfbacks usually gain the most yards and score the most touchdowns on a team. But they get hit hard and often. Halfbacks receive bruises as well as glory.

Fullback. Most of the time the fullback blocks for other players. But he sometimes runs with the ball, too. Fullbacks are usually bigger than halfbacks. They must be strong enough to block big defensive players and fast enough to run with the ball. Like halfbacks, they can also be used as pass receivers. The fullback is an important position.

Offensive formations get their names from the way the backs line up. In an I-formation, the fullback lines up behind the quarterback and the tailback lines up behind the fullback. The formation is shaped like a big "I" behind the line. In a "wishbone" formation, the fullback lines up behind the quarterback. The halfbacks line up behind and on both sides of the fullback. This formation is shaped like a turkey wishbone. Most pro teams use the T-formation. The "T" is formed by the halfback and fullback lining up next to each other a few yards behind the quarterback.

BILL WALSH ON PASSING

"It takes execution, timing, and touch to be a successful passer," said Bill Walsh, who coached Montana for most of his pro career. "You can throw too hard for a certain pass to be caught. It takes a player with the ability to know what type of pass needs to be thrown in certain situations."

Fullbacks need to be big and fast.

Receivers

The main pass receivers are the tight end, split end, and flanker. The tight end lines up next to one of the tackles. The split end lines up 5 to 7 yards outside the tackle on the other side. The flanker lines up outside the tight end and a few yards behind the line of scrimmage. Split ends and flankers are called wide receivers because they line up farther away from the rest of the team.

Wide receivers. The split end and the flanker have to be fast enough to outrun defensive backs. They also need to know how to intercept passes. They are usually good jumpers. To catch passes they often leap high over defensive backs.

Tight ends. Tight ends are bigger than wide receivers because they have to block big defensive linemen. But they also have to be fast so they can go out for passes. Tight end is one of the hardest positions to play in the NFL. Tight ends have to be both good pass receivers and good blockers.

Line

The offense must start every play with at least seven players on the line of scrimmage. The center plays in the middle of the line. On each side of him are the guards, tackles, and ends.

Center. The center starts every play by snapping the ball to the quarterback. This is usually done by handing the ball back between the center's legs to the quarterback. Sometimes the center will snap the ball back 5 to 7 yards to the quarterback. When the quarterback stands in the backfield to throw a pass, the formation is called a "shotgun." The center must also snap the ball back on punts and placekicks. The center blocks the player in front of him after he snaps the ball.

Guards. Guards line up on both sides of the center. Guards block either the player directly in front of them or a linebacker set a few yards back. Guards often have to "pull." That means they pull out of the line and cross behind the center to block the defensive player on the other side.

Tackles. Tackles line up next to the guards. They block on runs and on passes. On pass plays defensive players try to get past them to tackle the quarterback. Tackles almost always have a defensive player lined up opposite them. They usually don't pull out of the line the way guards do. They don't have to be as fast as guards. They need to be strong and heavy. Tackles are usually the biggest players on the team.

Offensive linemen are not allowed to hold their opponents. If they do, the offensive team receives a penalty. Defensive players can use their hands to grab blockers and throw them aside.

Defense

Unlike the offense, the defense does not have to put seven players on the line of scrimmage. Most defenses are either 4-3-2-2 or 3-4-2-2 formations. They are known more simply as "4-3" or "3-4" defenses. A 4-3 defense means there are four players on the line of scrimmage and three linebackers behind them. In a 3-4 defense, there are three

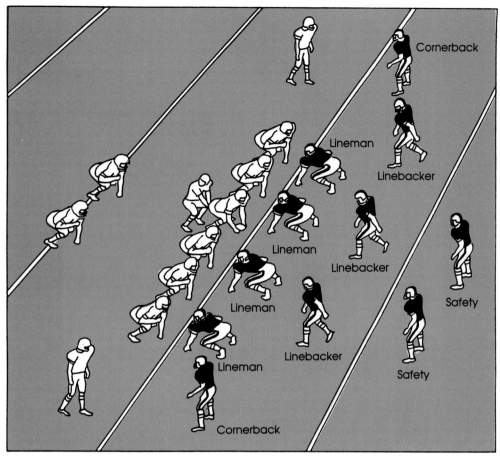

The 4-3-2-2 defense formation: Four players are on the line. Three linebackers are behind them. Cornerback lines up at each corner of the formation. Safeties stand farthest back.

players on the line and four linebackers behind them. Both the 4-3 and 3-4 formations have four defensive backs in the backfield, also called the secondary. They are the two cornerbacks and the two safeties. Cornerbacks line up at the corners of the formation. The safeties stand farthest from the line to make sure nobody gets by them and scores a touchdown.

Defensive ends. The two defensive ends line up opposite the offensive tackles. They try to tackle the runner and rush the passer. There is lots of body contact between defensive ends and offensive tackles. That is why defensive ends are big and strong. But they also have to be lean and quick so they can run after the ballcarrier. It

Ballcarrier attempting to break through line

helps if they are tall, too. That helps them knock down passes when they rush the quarterback.

Defensive tackles or **nose tackles.** In a 4-3 defense the two tackles play opposite the offensive guards. In a 3-4 defense with three defensive players on the line, there is only one tackle. He plays in the middle on the "nose" of the center. Tackles on defense are there to keep the offense from running up the middle. Tackles have to be strong so charging offensive linemen will not push them back.

Linebackers

Inside linebackers or **middle linebackers.** These are the linebackers who play behind the middle of the defensive line. In a 3-4 defense with four linebackers, the two inside linebackers play opposite the offensive guards a few steps back from the line. In a 4-3 defense with three linebackers, the middle linebacker plays opposite the center a few steps back. These linebackers are usually the best tacklers on the team. Their job is to tackle running backs coming through the middle and cover them when they go out for passes. On some pass plays linebackers blitz the quarterback.

Outside linebackers. Outside linebackers line up outside the defensive ends a few steps back from the line of scrimmage. They guard against the outside run. On passing plays they either cover one of the receivers or rush the quarterback. Outside linebackers have to be big and fast. They make a lot of tackles in the open field. Many of the game's biggest defensive stars, like Lawrence Taylor and Cornelius Bennett, play outside linebacker.

Defensive Backs

Defensive backs defend against pass receivers and ballcarriers who break through the line. They have to be quick, have good hands, and be good tacklers.

Cornerbacks. Cornerbacks play a few steps outside and behind outside linebackers. Cornerbacks do not need to be big, but they do need to be very fast to cover wide receivers. They have to be able to keep up with them when they suddenly change direction. Sometimes cornerbacks run backward so they can keep their eyes on the ball and the receiver.

Cornerbacks must be able to intercept passes and tackle pass receivers after they catch the ball. On running plays they need to come up and tackle the ballcarrier. In the NFL, cornerback is probably the hardest defensive position to play. With so many good passers and receivers cornerbacks have a tough job.

Safeties. There are two kinds of safeties—strong and free. The strong safety defends mostly against the run. The free safety defends mostly against the long pass. If the runner gets by the other players, the safety has to make the tackle. If a pass receiver slips by his defender, the safety has to cover him. A mistake by a safety can mean a touchdown for the other team.

Sometimes the team on offense is losing badly. It needs to pick up long yardage to make a first down. So it has to throw a long pass. To defend against a long pass, the defense will sometimes send in an extra back. A lineman is taken out to make room for the extra defensive back. The extra back is called a nickel back because he then becomes the fifth defensive back.

◀ Pass receivers must concentrate. "Once the ball's thrown to me, I don't hear anything," says San Francisco 49er's Jerry Rice. "No footsteps, no crowd. And I don't see anything except the ball."

CHAPTER

5

PLAYING TECHNIQUES

A good stance is important. The player who lines up in a proper stance will be quicker and better balanced than an opponent in a poor stance. There are three basic stances—the two point, three point, and four point. Football players should know how to line up in all three.

Two-Point Stance

Players in a two-point stance line up without their hands touching the ground. Running backs in an I-formation, wide receivers, linebackers, and defensive backs use the two-point stance.

If you are a running back, stand with your feet even. Lean slightly forward. Place your hands on your knees. Keep your head up and look straight ahead.

If you are lining up as a wide receiver, move your outside foot (the one nearest the sideline) back a little. Bend your knees and lean forward. Dangle your arms at your sides.

If you play linebacker, put your feet as far apart as your shoulders. Bend your knees. Keep your hands in front of you to fight off opposing blockers.

If you are a defensive back, have your outside front foot directly under your chin. Be ready to push off when the ball is snapped.

Two-point stance   Three-point stance   Four-point stance

Three-Point Stance

Offensive and defensive linemen, tight ends, most running backs, and some wide receivers use the three-point stance. To get into a three-point stance, start with your feet as far apart as your shoulders. If you are a running back, start with your feet even. If you are a lineman, move your right foot back a little. Bend forward and rest your left forearm (if you are right-handed) on the inside of your left thigh. With your right hand reach down and put your fingertips on the ground several inches in front of you. Keep your back straight and even with the ground. Your head should be up.

Four-Point Stance

The four-point stance is like the three-point stance, except that both your hands touch the ground. The four-point stance is used when the offense needs a burst of power forward to gain a couple of yards.

Whichever stance you use, do not let the other team know what you are going to do. Do not look in the direction you're going to go in before the ball is snapped. Always keep your head up and look straight ahead.

OFFENSE

Quarterbacks, running backs, and receivers need to know how to pass, catch, and run with the ball. Offensive linemen hardly ever touch the ball. Their job is to block for the ballcarrier.

Passing

The quarterback's most important job is to pass the ball. If you want to be a quarterback, you have to learn how to throw a spiral. That means throwing the ball overhand so it spins through the air with the nose of the ball straight.

To get a good grip on the ball, hold it near the back with your fingers spread out. Put your index finger across a seam near the top of the ball. Then hold the ball with two hands. Keep your left hand under the ball and bend your legs. As you step forward, point your front foot toward your target. As you throw, bring your arm and shoulder forward as if you are throwing a baseball. Follow through so your fingers end up pointing at your target.

The forward pass

Practice getting a good grip. Buffalo Bills quarterback Jim Kelly met his boyhood idol Terry Bradshaw when Kelly was 11 years old. Bradshaw had won four Super Bowls with the Pittsburgh Steelers. He showed Kelly how to hold the ball. Kelly thought he was the only kid in the world who knew the Bradshaw grip. But it did not feel right, so he eventually abandoned it. Today he uses a grip that is more comfortable.

In the old days quarterbacks used to hold the ball down near their waist before bringing it up to throw. Joe Namath, who led the New York Jets to a Super Bowl victory in 1969, changed that. Namath

liked to hold the ball up next to his ear. That way he could throw it quicker. Passing that way might feel uncomfortable to you at first, but it could make you a better passer.

Take the time to find the grip and throwing motion that is right for you. "The mechanics have to be right before you can work on consistency," says Warren Moon. Moon passed for over 40,000 yards with the Houston Oilers in the NFL and with Edmonton in the Canadian Football League.

Running

Running with the football is a natural talent that is hard to teach. Good runners follow their blockers, avoid tacklers, and learn from experience. However, all successful running backs need to learn how to take a handoff and catch a pitchout and pass.

Pitchout

A pitchout from the quarterback should arrive about waist high. As soon as you catch the ball, tuck it in your outside arm. Fumbling is the biggest mistake a running back can make, so hang on to the ball as tightly as you can.

Run hard at all times. Be willing to run over tacklers if you have to, but it is better to avoid them whenever possible. Jim Brown, the former Cleveland Browns Hall of Fame running back, said, "If I had a choice of running around you, or over you, I'd go around you. I wanted the yards, not to prove my manhood."

Catching

Running backs, ends, and flankers need to know how to catch the ball. Always catch a ball with your hands, not your body.

If the pass is level with your chest or higher, reach up and make a pocket with your thumbs and forefingers. If the pass is lower, put your pinky fingers next to each other and cup your hands. If the pass is below your waist, try to keep your elbows together, too. Your pinkies should also be together when you catch a pass over your shoulder.

◄Jim Kelly, quarterback of the Buffalo Bills, is looking for an open receiver.

Handoff

Most running plays begin with a handoff from the quarterback to a running back. When you receive a handoff, make a pocket with your arms. Hold the elbow closest to the quarterback up, and place your lower hand across your stomach with your palm up. When the quarterback puts the ball in the pocket you have made with your arms, clamp down on it. Keep the ball in both your arms until you cross the line of scrimmage. When you get into the open, put the ball in your arm closest to the sideline, and run as fast as you can.

Handoff

Pass Routes

Receivers run pass routes, or patterns. That is the way they try to get away from defenders. A receiver runs a square out pattern by running straight down the field, then cutting at a 90-degree angle toward the sideline. On a square in, the receiver cuts in toward the middle of the field.

A receiver running a slant runs out straight, then makes a 45-degree cut either in or out. The slant is like the square out, but the cut is not as sharp. On a hook, the receiver runs 10 yards, then turns back toward the quarterback. On a fly pattern, the receiver runs straight down the field as fast as he can.

The most important thing to remember when running pass routes is to make sharp cuts. That makes it harder for a defender to stay close to you.

Blocking is key to a successful ▶
run through the line.

40

Always keep your eye on the ball. When you catch the ball, tuck it in your arm nearest the sideline. Don't think about running with the ball until you catch the pass and put it securely away.

Catching takes hours of practice between a receiver and quarterback. "For every pass I caught in a game," said Hall of Fame end Don Hutson, "I caught 1,000 passes in practice." Hutson caught about 488,000 passes in practice with the Green Bay Packers from 1935 to 1945.

Blocking

There are two types of blocking—blocking for a run and for a pass. Every offensive player must block at least some of the time. The five interior linemen block on every play.

If you are an interior lineman, fire out at the defensive lineman or linebacker directly in front of you. Try not to make contact with your head first. Make contact with your shoulder near your opponent's waist. Bring your hands up to steer the defender away from the play. Do not grab—there is a penalty for grabbing on offense.

Pass protection takes more teamwork. The five linemen usually drop back together a few yards after the ball is snapped. Each pass blocker must block the defensive player who rushes into his area. When pass blocking, bend your knees and keep your hands up in front of you. Shuffle your feet to the right or left to keep the pass rusher away from the quarterback.

Anthony Munoz, a 10-time Pro Bowl offensive tackle with the Cincinnati Bengals, believes blockers should always attack, even on passing plays. "Why sit back and let a defensive player attack you the whole game while you react to his motions? Why not attack him the whole game and make him react?"

DEFENSE

Tackling

The most important job for the defense is to tackle the ballcarrier. Tackling is like blocking, except a tackler is allowed to use his hands to grab the ballcarrier. When you get ready for a tackle, bend your knees and keep your head up. Drive your shoulder (never your head) into the ballcarrier. Wrap your arms around him as you keep driving with your legs. You may not be able to take the runner down by yourself. But at least you will stop him or slow him down until you get help from your teammates.

Defensive players need to learn how to avoid blockers so they can make tackles. They can grab blockers and throw them aside, or they can push them back. Linebackers and defensive backs try to move out of the way so the blockers will miss them completely.

Pass Defense

Man-to-man pass defense is very important for defensive backs and linebackers. Backpedaling is a way to keep a receiver from getting behind you. When covering a receiver, stay close to him and wait for him to cut. After he makes his cut, stay as close as you can. You are not allowed to touch the receiver before he touches the ball. Try to knock the ball down so he cannot catch it. If the ball comes near you, try to intercept it. Never bat the ball up in the air. That gives the receiver a second chance to catch it.

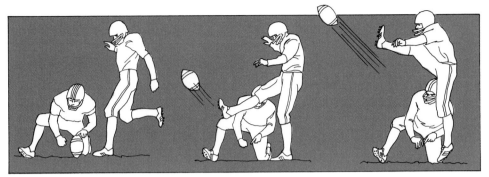

KICKING

Placekicking

Kicking is the closest football gets to its soccer roots. Many place-kickers are former soccer players. Today most placekickers use a style called soccer-style kicking.

A soccer-style kicker approaches the ball from the side. The ball is either on a tee (for kickoffs) or is held by a teammate (for field goals and extra points). To kick soccer-style, stand at a 45-degree angle to the ball. Your hips should face the ball. Strike the ball with the inside of your foot about an inch below the center. Follow through with your leg and body toward the target. When kicking the ball from behind, stand directly in back of the ball, and strike it with your foot.

Whichever style you use, always keep your head down and your eye on the ball. Distance means nothing if the ball does not go between the goalposts.

Punting

A good punter kicks the ball high and far. A punter does not use a holder or tee. He kicks the ball by dropping it out of his hands.

The first thing a punter needs to do is receive the snap from the center. As you wait for it, hold your hands palms up, pinky fingers close together. After you catch it, turn the ball so the laces face up. Then hold the back of the ball with your right hand and extend your arms. Your left hand should rest lightly on the side of the ball. Take two steps forward, drop the ball, and kick it as hard as you can.

WHERE TO PLAY FOOTBALL

Most young players get introduced to football by playing touch football. They may play in a park or lot or on a street with no traffic. In touch football, the defense only needs to touch the player who has the ball. The game may be one-handed or two-handed touch. The defensive player has to touch the ballcarrier with one or two hands to end the play.

Touch football is almost all passes. Once in a while, a trick running play gets mixed in. There is almost no play at the line. One of the pass rushers will count to 10 before he goes after the quarterback. All the offensive players except the quarterback run out for a pass.

Flag football is similar to touch, except the defense must pull a flag from the ballcarrier's belt or pocket to end the play. There is more running in flag football than in touch football.

Pop Warner Leagues are divided into 8 age and weight divisions. They are for young players 7 to 15 years old. The Leagues were named after the legendary coach, Pop Warner. He coached college football in the early part of the century. Pop Warner Leagues have sent John Elway, Lynn Swann, Joe Thiesmann, Randall Cunningham, Boomer Esiason, Steve Owens, Charles White, and others into stardom in college and the NFL. Pop Warner Leagues are in 38 states and have even spread to Mexico and Japan. The leagues have play-offs and a national championship game at the end of every season.

If you can't locate a Pop Warner League team near your home, contact the national headquarters for information. Write to:

Pop Warner Little Scholars, Inc.
920 Town Center Drive, Suite I-25
Langhorne, PA 19047-1748
Tel: (215) 752-2691

Now you should have a better idea of how to play football. As you can see, the game takes lots of dedication. But it is also fun. For all the hours you put in running, blocking, tackling, and sweating, always remember football is just a game. Do not get so caught up in winning that you forget to enjoy the sport. If football cannot be played with sportsmanship, it should not be played at all.

It is important to listen to your coach, just as it is important to listen to your parents and teachers. Coaches can teach you skills and give you the discipline you need to play and enjoy football.

Shaking hands at the end of the game is a sign of good sportsmanship.

GLOSSARY

Blitz: Pass rush of the quarterback by a linebacker or defensive back

Block: A hit by an offensive player to keep a defender from tackling the ballcarrier

Center snap: The center hands the ball between his legs to the quarterback to start an offensive play

Clipping: Blocking from behind

Defense: The team without the ball that is trying to stop the team with the ball

Drive: An offensive series of plays. A scoring drive ends in a touchdown or field goal.

End zone: The 10-yard area behind the goal line. A ballcarrier must reach the end zone to score a touchdown.

Extra point: A kick through the goalpost after a touchdown. Extra points can also be gained by a run or pass over the goal line following a touchdown.

Field goal: A kick from the playing field that goes between the goalposts for 3 points

First down: The first play in a series of four downs. The offensive team must gain 10 yards during the series to keep possession of the ball. When it gains 10 yards, it is rewarded with a first down and starts over.

Flag football: A playground game in which defensive players pull flags from the ballcarriers' belt or pocket instead of tackling

Fly pattern: A pass pattern in which the receiver runs straight down the field

Four-point stance: A stance which has a player start with both hands touching the ground in front of him

Fumble: A play in which the ballcarrier drops the ball before being tackled. The team whose player recovers the fumble gets possession.

Goal Line: The yard lines at both ends of the field 100 yards apart. They must be crossed to score a touchdown.

Goalposts: Posts at the back of the end zone. Teams must kick the ball between them for extra points and field goals

Holding: Grabbing a player. An offensive player gets a penalty when he holds his opponent.

I-formation: An offensive formation in which running backs line up in an "I" behind the quarterback

Illegal procedure: A play in which an offensive player moves forward before the ball is snapped. There is a penalty for it.

Incomplete pass: A pass not caught by offense or defense. The ball is marked down back at the line of scrimmage.

Interception: The catching of a pass by a defensive player. It gives his team the ball.

Kickoff: A kick that starts each half and follows every touchdown and field goal

Line of scrimmage: The yard line where each play begins

Man-to-man defense: A pass defense where all linebackers and defensive backs are assigned a specific receiver to cover

Nickel back: A fifth defensive back who comes into the game on passing downs

Offense: The team that has the ball

Officials: People who police the game and enforce the rules. They are usually dressed in striped shirts.

Offsides: Lining up beyond the ball. There is a penalty for being offsides.

Overtime: An extra period used to break ties

Pass interference: Hitting a receiver before he touches the ball. A defensive player receives a penalty for interfering with a pass.

Penalty: Punishment when a player breaks a rule. The team receiving the penalty may be punished by a loss of 5, 10, or 15 yards.

Punt: A kick by the offense to give up the ball, usually on the fourth down

Quarter: A fourth of the game. Each game is divided into four quarters. In college and the NFL each quarter is 15 minutes long.

Referee: The head official on the field

Sack: A tackle of the quarterback behind the line of scrimmage before he can throw a pass

Safety: Two points scored by the defensive team when they tackle a ballcarrier behind his goal line

Secondary: The part of the defense that includes cornerbacks and safeties

Shotgun: An offensive formation in which the quarterback lines up about 7 yards behind the center instead of directly behind him

Slant: A pass pattern in which the receiver runs straight down, then cuts across the middle of the field at a 45-degree angle

Soccer-style kicker: A kicker who kicks the ball from the side rather than from behind

Special teams: Teams that are sent into the game for kicking plays

Square out, or square in: A pass pattern in which the receiver runs straight down, then cuts toward the sideline or the middle of the field at a 90-degree angle

Sweep: A running play in which the ballcarrier runs around the end behind his blockers

T-formation: Offensive formation in which the backs line up in a line behind the quarterback, forming the letter *T.*

Three-point stance: A stance which has a player start with one hand on the ground

Touch football: A game of football in which the defense only has to touch the ballcarrier, not tackle him

Touchdown: Six points scored when the offense runs into the end zone or catches a pass or recovers a fumble in the end zone

Turnover: A fumble or interception that allows the defense to gain possession

Two-point stance: A stance which has a player start without either hand on the ground

Wishbone: Offensive formation with the fullback right behind the quarterback and two halfbacks behind him on each side

Zone defense: Pass defense in which defenders cover an area of the field rather than a specific receiver

FURTHER READING

Allen, James. *Football-Play Like a Pro*. Troll Associates, 1990

Doroska, Lud and Schiffer, Dorothy. *Football Rules in Pictures*. Perigree Books, 1991

Duden, Jane and Osburg, Susan. *Football*. MacMillan, 1991

Lorimer, Lawrence T., and Devaney, John. *Football Book*. Random House, 1989

Namath, Joe. *Football for Young Players and Parents*. Simon & Schuster, 1987

INDEX